GOD'S POCKET DICTIONARY

JIM YOUNG
Author
AWARE IN A WORLD ASLEEP

To Bill and Lori —

You bring many clients
to all you touch!

Love and hugs,

Jim :)

GOD'S POCKET DICTIONARY

Published by: creationspirit.net

ISBN: 144-997-4198
EAN-13: 9781449974190

Printed: United States of America

I do not really give you
new commands;
I have so few to give.
Only I tell them
in different ways
so as you teach others
you can reach people
with similar needs
who discern
in their own ways.

Jim Young
AS IF FROM GOD

Introduction

Nearly two decades ago, during what was to become a "second phase" of a life given to spiritual writing, I suddenly was "called" to my computer. For what, I knew not what. But since abiding a particular prayer method* I had learned to surrender to such calls to action, and I had a sense that this one would also serve some spiritual purpose. Setting aside another commitment, I dutifully arrived in the lap of what I have come to call my Muse.

"Put your hands on the keys of your laptop." I did as instructed. In a very short time, I "heard" a word, in this case, "tree." I typed "tree" as I heard it, and then simply waited. A few seconds later, my fingers appeared to move themselves across the keyboard, and this came out on the screen, even in the form shown here:

tree

**that which gives
root to Truth
anchored
in the everyday world.**

To put it mildly, I was astonished! Never before had I even entertained the idea of such inscription. In a moment or two, another word appeared, followed by yet another brief poetic phrase—and another, and another, still. In a little more than an hour, over fifty of these treats came onto the screen, guided by a Source that I was familiar with from engaging the earlier prayer method. All throughout this eerie experience, I felt a certain connection with a whisper of a voice discerned inwardly. Lodged still in that serene abode, I asked what these inspirational pieces were to be. Ask and you shall receive, it is said, so I ask I did. I received what I perceived to be a title for this collection: God's Pocket Dictionary. When I recovered from my momentary lapse into hilarity, I realized that the collection certainly spoke from a very different perspective than the ordinary.

From time to time after this initiatory episode, more and more entries were served up for inclusion. Then, one day, just as suddenly as this process had begun, I felt the direction to let it go, and I knew that eventually it would find its way to a publisher. Since then, the text has waited for just the right opportunity, which, as you now know, has found itself as a published book.

So ends this tale of how I came to discern spiritual guidance, simply by responding faithfully to the inner calling, day-by-day, moment-by-moment. Indeed, I am grateful for the opportunity to serve Life this way!

Jim Young

AS IF FROM GOD, by Jim Young

GOD'S POCKET DICTIONARY

flower

a blossom of My smile
on the stem of your heart
from the seed of your soul.

grave

a place bodies go to rest
while their Spirits
dance with Me
through the Universe.

limitation

the cramp of the planet
on the soul of the Universe
in the heart of humankind.

JIM YOUNG
Author
AWARE IN A WORLD ASLEEP

admonition

if I put My head
on your shoulders
you wouldn't be
you.

answer

My voice you hear
in the land
and its people
responding
to heartfelt need.

annihilation

**unfocused attention
on the rights
of privilege
and its
responsibilities.**

art

**the means
of awakening
My presence
in the human heart.**

beauty

that which frees
itself
from the hearts
of those
who open themselves
to My ways.

beggar

someone who
asks you
to forget
who you're
not.

blame

**an ugly flower
river askew
all sunsets the same
a gift unwanted
from Me to you.**

books

**ways of reaching
people
with similar needs
who need to hear
about them
in different ways.**

boat

the carrier
of emotions
along the stream
of Life.

bridge

the feeling
of connectedness
that comes
from knowing
that a heart
filled with joy
yesterday
can be your Truth
tomorrow
by faith expressed
today.

candle

**My Light displayed
lifting one's Soul
to the heavens.**

cathedral

**an open heart
and mind
at One with Me
intending only Love.**

children

**My gifts
to begin
again and again
learning what love
truly is.**

church

whoever uses
this key
opens the door
to eternal prosperity.

control

**going nowhere
with a grip on Life
when letting go
opens the gifts
of the Universe.**

courage

the gift
of inner Truth
one gives to self
on the journey
of relationship
with Me.

cross

the burden you bear
when you carry Me
to others
'tis but a feather
on the winds
of heaven.

****

passion for Me
expressed
as compassion
for all that is.

death

a retainer of the past
grounded
in the Truth
of our Oneness
now.

debris

painful memories
absorbed long ago
and far away
returned now
to their senders
wrapped in peace.

disappointment

**choices reflecting
lack of gratitude
and understanding
that My love
for humankind
is endless.**

Eucharist

broken bread
and outpoured wine
being One
every day
in each
relationship.

evil

anxiety is that
doubt is that
all relatives of fear
are that:
all divisive thoughts
in their ways
of working
against love.

expectation

how are you
packaged?
in a little brown bag
of everyone else's
views of you
re-wrapped now
in this
understanding.

failure

a relationship
unfulfilled
a flower's fragrance
wasted
a heart contained.

faith

what is rendered
unnecessary
when centered
in the presence
of unfettered Love.

fear

that which
paralyzes Life
and the freedom
I give Life.

fire

**a heart aflame
giving birth to Life
as one's gift
of enthusiasm.**

flower

a blossom
of My smile
on the stem
of your heart
from the seed
of your Soul.

frame

**etching My image
on the lining
of your heart
wherever it appears.**

friend

as a tree
gives blossoms
the nourishment
for Life
I give to you
My life everlasting.

future

**living an illusion
of the past
as a wish for
a better tomorrow
when the best
is with Me
now.**

game

**what you play
to avoid expressing
what you
really are.**

genius

inspiration
demonstrated;
imagination
acknowledged
and accepted
fertilized
and grown
into the material.

gentle

breeze-tossed hair
tear-caressed cheek
My whispers
in your heart.

gift; giving

you are that
in ways
you do not know;
accept yourself
as gift
joyfully now
and cast
your wrapping
aside.

****

the release
of your ownership
on My treasures
for the world.

****

what is life?
what are you?
the very same.
gift is gift.

gold

**a loving heart
transforming
hate
and injustice.**

grace

**My kiss of Light
on the darkness
that clouds
your heart
from the Truth
that is you.**

grandchildren

**My way
of sending love
with all
the judgment
removed.**

grave

a place bodies
go to rest
while their Spirits
dance with Me
through
the Universe.

guiltless

giving like the early
morning dew
to the blades
of grass:
without concern
for the result.

home

when your
heart
is at peace
anywhere is.

hug

the unmistakable
imprint of love
that seals
a relationship
with trust.

hurry

missing My gifts
which soften
an angry
and un-for-giving
world.

illness

**leaving what I Am
and all you are
dismissed from view.**

illusion

**if I wanted you
to be something
other than human
why then
did I create you
as human?**

intellect

a servant
to the Truth
that is you.

interdependence

**Our hands
and hearts
interlocked
for the good of all.**

joy

**releasing your heart
to love as I love
with the very same
results.**

judgmental

the need
to have all
be like you
when all
are really Me.

kiss

**the brush
of an angel's wing
upon your heart.**

laughter

**My heart
crying out
unabashedly
for your joy.**

lavishly

**giving
your heart
as I give
in all circumstances.**

leadership

**taking others
to the threshold
of their own
Truth
and Power.**

likeness

giving root
to the fruit
of being
in the image
of Me.

limitation

the cramp
of the planet
on the soul
of the Universe
in the heart
of humankind.

love

as in the beauty
of the snowflakes;
in as many ways
as they are
with the gentleness
of their kiss
upon your cheek.

****

that which
lies before you
in the likeness Me.

****

**fields
of spring flowers
in the warmth
of your smile.**

marriage

**a joining
of What I Am
with all that Is.**

message

whisper
stubbed toe
seeming disaster:
all roots of change.

mind

writing down
and saying
everything
that comes
to thought
because
that's the way
ego-mind likes it;
live Me instead.

mistake

unknowing
unaware
uncaring
asleep.

music

heavenly notes
floating 'round
and 'round
a flute kissing
your ears
sweet voices
taming your heart
healing you
yet again.

name

those labels
put on others
when peeled away
let you
see Me in all.

never

**the disappearance
of My love for you;
unforgiveness;
My failure
to respond
to your heartfelt
need.**

nourishment

food for the body;
caring from Me
for the elements
of Soul.

opposite

**a controlling hand
from a loving heart;
sweet fruit
from a choked
and twisted tree;
closeness to Me
in a lifeless world.**

past

a life lived
anywhere
but in My presence.

peaceful

**what your mind
becomes
when your heart
is filled
with the fullness
of Our relationship.**

perfection

**the juice
of an orange
the bud of a rose
a blade of grass
and you.**

photo

**a mirror
of My image
upon your Soul.**

poetry

demonstrating
Me
through all you are
and do.

poverty

mired in the muck
of self-importance
instead
of flowing
like the wine
of compassionate
love.

practice

seeing Me
in all
smiling at Me
in all
your heart changing
steadily
becoming
Love for always.

prayer

being only
what you already
are
in all you say
and do.

punishment

frozen emotions
a mountain unseen
a lover mis-taken
Our love amiss.

purpose

I died
not on the cross;
Life was given.
I suffered not on the
cross;
My passion
and compassion
gave meaning to life.

****

living
the highest order
like plants
in spite of our ego
telling us
otherwise.

quality

**living true
to the Essence
Life is
no matter
what the turmoil.**

resurrection

Life's treasures
given away
you travel now
with Me
into the inner depths
of Understanding;
death
rebirth
over and again
you picture
transcendence.

risk

**trusting the potential
of your heart
in My hands
freeing all.**

rope

stands
of episodes
woven together
demonstrating
Life's purpose
from end to end.

ruler

**a measure of love
for what is
Mine.**

security

the assurance that
with Me
you can handle
anything
that comes your way.

simple; simplicity

passionate love
for Me
compassionate love
for others;
broken bread
and outpoured wine.
do this
in remembrance
of Me.

****

love Me
and not other gods
follow Me
and not other gods
not yourself
or others
or things
just Me.

song

song
what is song?
angels' wings
wafting
My heart-filled
voice.

spine

**support for Life
as yet
unfulfilled.**

stone

**that which
a heart turns into
when love's
in difference.**

strength

awash with tears
compassion felt
giving to another
what one
wants to keep.

taste buds

often expressed
as ego
of the mouth.

tears

the release
of Soul's
pain
wrapped
in My joy for you.

time

**what
you feel
when you forget
that Life's
the present
in which
to simply Be.**

tool

**Truth and Justice
and Mercy:
My vehicles for
working miracles
while evil
brings death
into Life.**

touch

**My way
of reminding you
of My presence;
a smile the same.**

transportation

**ways of getting you
from there
to Here
now.**

tree

**that which gives
root to Truth
anchored
in the
everyday world.**

unburdened

**wiping stress away
with love
for what Life
teaches you.**

understanding

**an inner knowing
that
the manifestations
of earthly Life
are but the mirrors
of your Soul.**

****

**that which renders
forgiveness
unnecessary.**

victim

frailty
and low self-worth
disguised
as love of self.

walk

the way
of the journey
that is you.

wealth

the abundance
of all I Am
like a flower
releasing
its fragrance.

weapon

a gentle tone
a tender touch
a smiling face
an open heart
a warm embrace
acceptance.

will

**My heartfelt desire
for your
heartfelt needs
expressed
as Ours.**

wine

**passionate love
from the winepress
of My heart
flowing as
compassion
from the depths
of yours.**

wisdom

**the gift
of knowing
the Truth
of your journey.**

work

awake
in the demonstration
of the gift
you are
to all that Is.

worth

embracing what
you know
is Truth for you
rather than
sinking to the depths
of another's
view of you.

****

living lavishly
as I know you to be
in the likeness of Me.

xenophobe

**blind
to My likeness
in all.**

you

this
who expresses
in My hand;
this
who laughs
in My voice;
this
whose Life
demonstrates
My soul!

youth

**unabashed
enthusiasm
for the Eternity
each one is.**

zebra

**My metaphor
for human
intolerance
of ambiguity.**

NOW IT'S YOUR TURN!

Part of the reason for putting this book before you is to assist you in developing spiritual listening skills. Now you have the opportunity to see how well you can listen **inwardly**. Very simply, sit in silence and listen for a word that comes seemingly out of nowhere. Write it down, either on these next few pages or on your computer screen. Then, listen for the still, small voice that will provide the spiritual meaning of the word you heard earlier. You may need to ask that very question: what spiritual meaning does this word have for me? Then, listen. When you've heard the definition from within, and **not by thinking about it**, record the definition alongside the word.

When you have done that, you get a prize. As the definitions from you and other "listeners" arrive, I'll draft a Listener's Edition to God's Pocket Dictionary and see that it's published, citing each person for their contribution. Merely send your definition (you can submit up to two) and the information requested below to me through the email address on my website, **or** fill in the information requested below, and then cut the next two pages out of the book and send them to me at the address posted there.

Most importantly, simply have fun listening inwardly. As you become more spiritually aware, you life will brighten beyond belief. Go to it!

My Spiritual Definition

Word:

Definition:

Name:

Address:

Email:

Phone:

Send to:
Jim Young
Listeners' Version
PO Box 43
Beaver, AR 72613

OR

Via email to the address at:
www.creationspirit.net

OTHER BOOKS BY JIM YOUNG

(See **www.creationspirit.net**
for descriptions)

Aware in a World Asleep

As if from God

On Making Love; Spiritual
Testimony to the Gift Life Is

Real Life Leadership in a
Newfangled World; The Es-
sential Remedy for a Symp-
tomatic Society

What If...? Changing Your
Life to Fit Your Truth

Consider the Source; Rising
Above Illusion Into the Light
of Truth

The Creation Spirit; Express-
ing Your Divinity in Every-
day Life

A Labor of Love; Weaving
Your Own Virgin Birth on the
Loom of Life

Keys to the Door of Truth;
The Metaphysical Musings of
a Born-Yet- Again

Only Mind Matters; Emerg-
ing From the Waters of Sym-
bolic Meaning

E-Books
(Download:
<u>www.creationspirit.net</u>)

Thanks for the Yellow Roses

God's Pocket Dictionary

More on Making Love

As If From God, Too

Spirit Noodles

Swimming with the
Mosquitoes

From Human Doing to
Spiritual Being

The Gospel of St. Thomas
Revealed as Spirit

Poetics Made Abundant

JIM YOUNG'S WEBSITE

<u>www.creationspirit.net</u> This
website contains additional
creations to come through
Jim Young, including e-books
and a link to his collector-
quality photography. Speak-
ing services and classes deal-
ing with Dr. Young'a writings
are also available.

4382805

Made in the USA
Charleston, SC
12 January 2010